GET WELL SOON!

A Practical Guide To Managing, Training And Entertaining
Your Dog While They Recuperate From Surgery

A Train Your Dog Guide™

Almudena Ortiz Cué,

M.A., CTC, CPDT-KA, Tellington Touch® cert.

Get Well Soon!
A Practical Guide To Managing, Training And
Entertaining Your Dog While They Recuperate From Surgery
A Train Your Dog Guide™

Copyright © 2018 by Almudena Ortiz Cué

Cover design and illustration by MACOR.
https://www.facebook.com/macordesigns/

ISBN 978-0-9978992-3-8

Published by:

C.H.A.C.O. Dog Training & Behavior Consulting LLC, publisher.
P.O. Box 454 Tesuque, NM 87574
www.chacodogtraining.com

To Laika (shown at left) and
Rioja (Rio) my two "girls" who
breezed through their recovery
with grace and patience.

"This wonderfully accessible guide by Ms. Ortiz Cué will not only help during the illness or surgery recovery period but is useful immediately for ANY dog, ANY time! Any veterinarian like myself knows the daunting task of insuring an animal has 'cage rest' for a medical or surgical recovery. This book is the answer to our prayers! Every dog parent will benefit from these techniques not only during the illness and post-operatively but for the entire life of the animal. Thank you for this much-needed guide!"

Dr. Dee Blanco, Santa Fe NM.

"Almudena has packed this book full of tips and tools to keep your dog mentally healthy during their crate rest, or limited activity phase of recovery. The pain of watching a restless dog try to recover from surgery is over! With this book, you'll know exactly how to keep your dog active in appropriate ways for recovery, and you'll learn about the technical aspects of dog training, which Almudena has broken down so that even the most beginner trainer can become a pro. Even if you're not scheduling surgery anytime soon, this book will give you and your dog plenty to chew on!"

Erica Beckwith CTC, CPDT-KA, Fear Free Certified Professional. A Matter of Manners Dog Training

Contents

Introduction

I BEGAN TO WRITE this guide while my dog Rioja was recuperating from surgery. Her surgery was a major one and it required 10-weeks of crate rest or immobility. Even for someone like me, who trains dogs for a living and has had two prior experiences with lengthy recoveries for my dogs, the idea of keeping our otherwise very healthy and active dog in a state of limited mobility was daunting.

We decided and move forward with the surgery as this would mean getting back, as soon as possible, to our fun life with Deuce (our male dog) and Rio. Besides, it made sense to get over the recuperation before winter to avoid the possibility of falls.

The questions I asked myself over and over at the beginning of our "adventure" included: How can I make Rio more comfortable, less bored, her life less limiting *while following all medical Veterinarian Surgeon (DVM) recommendations for a whole and speedy recovery?* This guide offers my answers to those challenges.

Among my coping strategies, I began to review various ways that I could set up our home so that Rio would not be isolated to one room or one crate, but rather remain part of family life as much as possible, while following our veterinarians (DVM) recommendations.

I am sharing strategies and ideas based on the recommendations of the two vets who operated on our dogs, Laika & Rio. I am surmising that when recuperating from any surgery, the recommendations might be very similar with perhaps the time of recovery being different in duration.

If anything in this guide contradicts what your vet recommends as to how to take care of your dog, *please* follow his/her advice and disregard my suggestions since doing otherwise is really not worth compromising your dog's well-being and recuperation.

Part of what I have learned in the post-surgery process is to think of myself as the "adult" and to make sure I do not succumb to my dog's desire to do as she pleases, such as: walking farther than she should at a given point during the recovery process. For example, in Rio's case, to not let her jump up on our bed because I feel bad for her now that she cannot snooze with us in the morning as she normally does.

Yes, of course, I feel sorry for her since her life, for the time being, is limited and she does not even understand why. But, we are the responsible caregivers—the "adults" (remember?). We are also committed to her overall well-being thus we make the choice(s) every day to follow along with what we know is best for her even if she has other ideas in mind.

Part of what will make your dog's recovery a success with as little impact as possible on both of your lives, is not only to be a responsible caretaker who makes good decisions for her, but also to plan ahead with as much empathy for your dog as you can muster.

Let me explain: as part of a good outcome, you also will have to make some sacrifices. You might have to re-arrange your schedule to supervise as much as possible, you might have to hire some competent help when it is not feasible for you to take care of your dog. Yes, you might also have to buy some stuff such as extra crates, a harness, toys, etc. You might have to remove some furniture and introduce into your otherwise perfect decor some ugly, bulky crate and x-pens to help you both sail smoothly through this taxing time.

Planning ahead: Not everyone will have the luxury of planning way ahead for the day their pup comes back home from surgery. If you can, this will be ideal. If your situation is one where the dog needs immediate surgery, just do the best you can to follow some or all of these recommendations. This is why I am writing this guide; so that you are not overwhelmed and pressed for time. You will, however; need to observe your dog carefully so that you can make sure your dog is comfortable and safe.

Almudena Ortiz Cué, M.A. CTC, CPDT-KA,
Tellington TTouch cert.
Tesuque, New Mexico. Summer, 2018

CHAPTER 1

How To Use This Guide

BEFORE WE START training, it is important to understand certain principles of animal learning as well as how to prepare for the sessions. We want these training sessions to be fun, efficient and effective.

How Dogs Learn

Dogs learn mainly in two ways:

1. Learning By Association (emotional response)
When the sound of the can opener signals that it's time to eat! This type of learning is called Associative learning or Pavlovian conditioning. In essence, what Pavlov was able to demonstrate

by pairing the sound of a bell—initially a neutral (irrelevant) stimulus to the dogs, with something that was very meaningful for them (their food) was that after a few pairings of the ringing of the bell *before* presenting the food, the dogs began to salivate at the sound of the bell in anticipation of food.

Sometimes associations are good, from the perspective of the dog, and sometimes they can be bad.

Now, salivation is not something that we can produce on cue, it is part the autonomic system so it happens on its own when the circumstances are right. In addition, associative learning has a strong bearing on emotions. We can teach our dogs to love certain things such as leashes, and can openers, because we have paired them with good stuff for our dogs in our daily lives.

2. Learning By Consequence

Learning by consequence is a little different than learning by association. When dogs are learning in this manner, they learn that their behavior carries consequences. If we are smart and we take advantage of this law of learning[1] and we begin to apply good consequences to our dog's behavior, our dog will offer the behavior we want more often.

Here is an example: You ask your dog to wait at the front door, your dog does so, and as a reward (also called a reinforcer) you open the front door for your dog. And off you go to your fun adventure! If, on the other hand, you ask your dog to wait and he rushes forward, you then gently close the door so that your

---

[1] Notice that I wrote *law* of learning which means it is not an opinion, but a law that governs how animals learn.

dog does not get to rush out and if your timing is correct, your dog will not be able to go past you. Thus, learning that moving forward before you release him will not pay off.

Another example: Your dog is holding in its mouth something your dog should not have; you have worked on this behavior because your dog loves to put items in her mouth. You ask your dog to release it by saying: *drop it* and your dog opens its mouth dropping the item. As a consequence, for doing what you asked the dog to do, you give your pup a rub on the belly and a tiny piece of cheese. As a result, your dog will learn that dropping stuff when you ask means good things for her, so she will do this more often.

In using this guide, you will learn and implement both types of learning. Your dog will begin to work with you because you are rewarding consequences for desired behavior.

We Don't Need No Stinkin' Leaders!

Please keep in mind that the way that you will be working with your dog through this program is by using what is called **Positive Reinforcement**. This means that we will mainly[2] use motivation and rewards for behaviors that we'd like to see more of. There is no intimidation, use of force or making the dog

---

[2] The other technique we will be using is what is called Negative Punishment, which means in the behavioral sciences the *removal* of something the dog wants, such as closing the door so that the dog cannot go out the door before being released. Please know that the use punishment does *not* mean hitting, scaring the dog; just the removal or loss of opportunity for reinforcement.

afraid, so that he complies with our request in the training. Remember: we want our dog to be a willing and enthusiastic participant in the training. In addition, we will not subscribe to the erroneous and over-simplified idea that we must be the "alpha" or the so-called *leader of the pack,* implying that our dog must obey our every request or else... This misconstrued idea is not based on the ethology of dogs. Moreover, it is abusive and uses fear and intimidation as strategies for surrender of the dog, instead of happy engagement of both parties. Rather, we will use our big mammalian brain and teach our dog that working with us means that he gets really good treats, attention, fun and games because all good things in your dog's universe come from you! And who does not like to be treated nicely, huh?

Additional Concepts To Keep In Mind

Now that you know how dogs learn, we will explore other concepts that will help you in training your dog.

As part of our training, we will use what is called a **clicker** so that we can specify to the dog with precision for which behavior deserves a treat. The clicker is not the reward; it is *the **marker*** that tells the dog a reward is coming. We can train without a clicker, but learning how to use one means

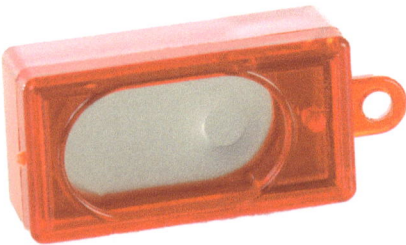

One kind of clicker: The "box" clicker.

that we can really focus on what we want to reinforce (pay the dog) for. As you will see, this will be the first training you will do with your dog.

What Kind Of Reward Should You Use?

Rewards are everywhere. They change constantly depending on what your dog is interested in at the moment.

Because your dog is not able to do much while in recovery, some rewards will be off limits. No rabbit chasing, jumping up and down with joy. Instead, you will be using food & treats, to pay your dog for a job well done.

Food is one of the most powerful rewards we can use for getting the behaviors that we want. It is a Primer reinforcer-something the dog wants or will work for. It is a Primary reinforcer because the dog does not need to learn to love food. However, reinforcers (or rewards) change all the time, so if your dog just had a great bowl of food, perhaps he'd rather take a nap than eat more food. In order to motivate our dog, we must use whatever the dog wants at the moment.

Using Food In Training

When using food as a reward it's important to *not* feed your dog in excess of his daily caloric intake; your dog will eat the same amount of food he eats because you will subtract your dog's daily food, and instead use some small, tasty treats to train. All dogs have individual preferences as to what they really love to get as a treat, but for the most part, dogs love to eat stuff that is soft and smelly, and not dry—such as dry milk bones. You can experiment if you do not already know what kind of food or treats your dog loves. Most dogs prefer something else other than their daily chow, but you can try and see if your dog will work for kibble (dry food), if so that is a good place to start.

If your dog's diet permits it, you can branch out and introduce some other tasty treats/food. Here is a list to get you started:

1   Turkey, beef or chicken, and hot dogs of good quality. Given in excess, I consider hot dogs as "junk food" and very high in fat so I do not use often.
2   Food rolls (lots of brands and variety).
3   Hard-boiled egg.
4   Small pieces of low-fat Mozzarella cheese.
5   Cheerios and popcorn—some dogs love these two.
6   Apple, carrot, sweet potato (No grapes or nuts of any kind!)
7   Prepackaged small training treats. My favorite: *Zukes, Real Meat*—again see what your dog loves.

Getting Started with Training

Ideally you can train your dog once or twice a day. I know, I know, you are probably thinking that you need to quit your job to fulfill this! Do not fret! When I suggest that you work with your dog once or twice a day, I am suggesting training sessions that will last at the most 5 minutes per session. See, you do not need to quit your job. Now that you have your treats and clicker ready, a hungry dog, and you have read this guide, it is time to train.

Gather all you need:

▸ Training plan(s) (provided)
▸ Treats
▸ Training form for note taking
  (optional, you can do this later)
▸ Clicker

It is always best to have all of the above items gathered and for you to decide where you will train *before* you go get your dog. Your dog must be comfortable, able to do the work and feel safe.

Nuts & Bolts Of Training

In order for your dog to learn, we need to set things up so that he is successful and gets rewarded for being so. This method of training will help you in keeping track of "correct" answers. Whatever we can measure, we can improve so that is why we will use the following tracking method to train. It is called the **PUSH, DROP, STICK,** (PDS) system. PDS is a system of counting the number of winning/losing trials (repetitions of a behavior) in a set so that we know if we need to stay at the current level of difficulty (stick), lower the criteria (drop), or raise the criteria (push). By **criteria,** I mean the precise and observable behavior that we are reinforcing. For example: A "sit-reinforce" is observed when the dog's butt hits the ground. The beauty of the PDS system is that you will also be providing feedback to your dog.

Push, Drop, Stick: How It Works

- ▶ You will work with your dog on a given behavior per the training plans provided here in 5 trial sets.
- ▶ Whenever your dog is successful, you will click and pay (give a treat/kibble).
- ▶ If your dog is *not* successful, you will make note of it and adjust the exercise to make it easier for your dog to succeed.
- ▶ Our goal is always to make things so easy for the dog that he is winning all the time.[3]
- ▶ Remember, the more we reinforce a behavior, the more we will see it in the future. Also, your dog's confidence will soar as he is being successful.
- ▶ If you asked for a behavior and your dog was successful, you will continue for 5 trials total at this stage of difficulty. If your dog makes a mistake or mistakes, you will follow the system below to move the training forward and to teach your dog how to learn what you want to teach him.

---

[3] When training advanced learners this changes, but for now we will keep things easy for your dog & you.

PDS:

1 If your dog gets four out of five or five out five correct responses, you **PUSH.**
2 If your dog gets one or two out of five correct responses, you **DROP.**
3 If your dog gets three correct response of five you **STICK.**

Three Different Strategies

In using this guide, you will use three different strategies for helping your dog learn. These are luring, shaping and capturing.

Luring: A hands-off method of guiding the dog through a behavior. For example: using a food lure to teach the dog to place its butt on the ground by raising the treat over the dog's head (dog's head goes up, butt goes down).

Shaping: Teaching by approximation. For example: teaching a dog to lie down by reinforcing when the dog lowers its head, shoulders, elbows, butt and finally the belly on the ground.

Capturing: Reinforcing a behavior when the dog exhibits the behavior. For example: reinforcing the dog for lying quietly on its bed.

Extinction: While your dog is learning new things, we want to pay for EVERY correct behavior. Once we are sure our dog has learned what we wish him to learn, we will only pay (give a treat) on occasion to avoid what is called "extinction." Laws of learning also tell us that whatever behavior is not reinforced (in some way) the behavior will stop taking place or become extinct. Avoid the newly acquired behavior to go into extinction by paying your dog on occasion once your dog can perform the behavior 10 out of 10 times or at least 9 out of 10 times. At this point in the learning process, the behavior will remain stronger if we pay only on occasion instead of every time as we did when the dog was just learning.

Mechanics In Dog Training

There are a lot of mechanical skills in training. These require practice. Ideally you will initially practice without your dog. Two mechanical skills that you need to master are:

1 The sequencing and timing of the click and treat (c/t).
   ▶ You *always* click **before** you treat or give any other reinforcer you are using.
   ▶ If you click by mistake (which you will; you're only human!) you still have to pay the dog. It is your mistake and we want to make sure the dog will associate the clicker with the reward— *"when they 'click' I get paid.* Awesome!"

2 Delivery of the food after the click.

- ► Remain as neutral as possible with no fussing before your dog has done the behavior that deserves the treat. Do not reach for the food just yet. Wait! Click with precision and then...
- ► Reach for the treat. This is important because we want to maintain in place the order of events: click *then* treat, Also, if you are moving your hand to get to the treat, this will distract your dog. We want a dog that is focused on us and what we are doing not the food that is coming his/her way.
- ► You may keep your treats in a fanny pack, training bag or even a dish next to you. Your choice.

Final Note

If you are in a rush or you are becoming frustrated with the training, please do *not* take it out on your dog. Instead, just put the dog away, regroup and try again later. This is one of the most salient mistakes people make when training their dog. Not only is it not fair to the dog (who is the learner, we are the teachers) but it will also set you back in the process.

CHAPTER 2

Keeping To Recommendations

ONE OF THE most difficult challenges about this period of recovery for your dog is to follow very closely all your veterinarian's medical recommendations. Think of your dog as having a team who is rooting for the best outcome possible. It is indeed a team effort. As my own veterinarian told me, 50% of the success of the operation depends on the post-op care at home. That is a whopping percentage in determining the success of the surgical procedure and your dog returning to a full life.

Much of this guide is designed to support you in doing just that. If you decide you can't or don't want to engage in the training with your dog, you will still get lots of benefit from **the**

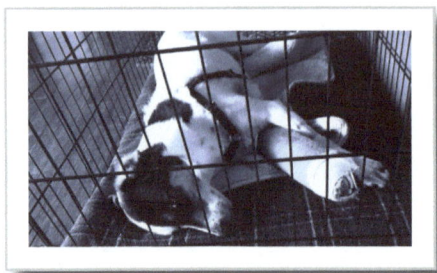

Rio relaxing in her crate.

post-operation management and **mental stimulation** recommendations in this guide.

None of my recommendations fall in the realm of medical advice, as I am a professional dog trainer and not a medical specialist.

As I mentioned in the introduction, they will however support you in following your veterinarian's advice.

What is Post-Operation Management?

It means controlling the environment so that your dog does not behave in a way that could risk the operation's outcome.

Of course, in the context of a post-op setting, management means that your dog will not engage in any activities that can hurt or compromise the operation for a determined length of time. Notice that I mentioned that we are controlling or managing the environment, not the dog per se. However, if you have a management plan in place and you follow it, your dog will by de facto not be able to engage in activities that can hurt the recuperation process. In the next chapter, we will explore environmental conditions to help with the management procedures which you will be required to do for as long as your DVM says they are needed.

CHAPTER 3

The At Home Set-up & Equipment Needed

IMAGINE BEING A *very* social animal, as dogs are, and having to spend countless hours for many days in isolation. This can be very aversive and depressing to most dogs. I have found that it's really hard on pet parents too because they are used to being around their dog on a daily basis as they enjoy many aspects of their life together. The suggestions below will allow for your dog to remain as much as possible an integral part of the family, while still being contained.

Choosing The Right Crate

Besides being crate trained, your dog **must** be able to do the following inside the crate:

- ▶ Stand up completely erect on all fours.
- ▶ Turn around.
- ▶ Lie down completely with extremities extended, if it wishes to do so.
- ▶ Be able to see outside the crate.

I prefer wired crates because they:

- ▶ come in many sizes that allow you to buy the one just right for your dog;
- ▶ give your dog the ability to see outside the crate;
- ▶ provide air circulation and
- ▶ allow you to easily check on your dog while he/she is in their crate

Confinement How To Do It Well

The most efficient way to keeping your dog quiet mentally and physically is the use of a crate. By now, most people are familiar with crates. However, what most people unfortunately do not know is that dogs need to be **crate trained.** The idea that all dogs love the crate because it's like a "den" to them is false.

In order for a dog to feel safe in a crate, it must be taught that the crate is a safe place. Some take to the idea with more ease than others; and for some dogs—especially if they have had a previous bad experience being crated will find getting into the crate an anxious experience. Forcing a dog to get into a crate without teaching the dog to be comfortable in it is frankly cruel and should be avoided.

If your dog is not crate trained, this is where you need to start. By crate trained I mean that your dog LOVES to spend time snoozing and hanging out in the crate on his/her own accord. You train your dog to go into its crate often just to do that: to stay calmly in the crate. If needed, your dog can also spend the whole night comfortably sleeping inside the crate. This training guide includes information as well as training plans to help with crate training.

X-Pens

If your dog is not crate trained and you must contain him ASAP, then get an X-pen. X-pens come in a variety of materials and sizes. Once again, the size of your dog will determine the X-pen you will choose. The X-pen, because of its configuration of modular panels, can be set up in almost any room in almost any config-uration possible. One should, of course, make sure that the dog cannot tip it over. Learning how to set them up correctly is a must but it is not rocket science. Some dogs are really good at jump-ing barriers, so if you suspect your dog might try to jump over

An X-pen has multiple panels that can be arranged in many configurations.

the X-pen, you must be hyper vigilant that the opportunity does not appear. Once they learn they can jump over the X-pen, it's much harder to keep them inside. Play it safe and get the tallest X-pen you can find. If your dog is large and prone to escaping, you might have to double up on the X-Pen's height as well.

Baby Gates

Ah, baby gates! Another wonderful tool that can make almost any room an appropriate containment area for your dog. I personally like baby gates that come with a door that let me easily enter and exit the pen rather than have to hop over the gate. I have found that it is mandatory to buy a baby gate that fits properly. Most baby gates expand to achieve multiple sizes. It's important to buy one that is of good quality. You need to be able to trust that your dog cannot jump or bulldoze through the gate when not being supervised, thus a secure baby gate is crucial.

The baby gates and X-pens can be the salvation tools to keep your dog in the proximity of the family as well as contained. True, your home will not look its best with a baby gate or X-pen in place, but you will feel so much better because your dog can remain with you and not be isolated.

A Word About Tying Your Dog To Furniture

This is where planning really pays off. I do not recommend attaching your pup to any piece of furniture when not being supervised. Your dog can chew at the furniture, and the furniture might not be as sturdy as you thought it was and now you have a dog dragging it or having the furniture fall on your dog. Only if you remain next to your dog, then having him attached to the furniture might be safe and a good option too.

CHAPTER 4

Mental Stimulation & Training Plans

NFORTUNATELY FOR DOGS, many dog *parents* aren't aware of the importance of mental stimulation for their dogs. I would argue that mental stimulation or the lack thereof wreaks havoc on most dog's lives. They either don't get enough mental stimulation or they are getting the wrong kind of stimulation, which can lead to over-stimulation and arousal. I am afraid you both will be crawling up the wall and your dog is not supposed to do that! You can take this opportunity to learn what your dog likes and how to provide this very important benefit of mentally and physically stimulating your dog.

Mental Stimulation

Mental stimulation can mean different things to different dogs. Just like some people enjoy reading, knitting, etc. as to what they find stimulating or interesting. There are always individual choices for dogs, but at the end of the day, *a dog is a dog, is a dog*. My recommendations are based once again on the ethology of dogs. In essence, *mental stim*. As it is known in the field of dog training, it subscribes to the importance of **daily** mental engagement for our pets. This holds true even if our dog is in recuperation. Of course, it is reasonable to curtail physical stimulation as needed when recuperating.

As a result of appropriate mental stimulation, your dog should be more content, tired and ready to settle. If your dog becomes too agitated—especially now that he is not supposed to be doing much physically you are either doing too much or your dog is perhaps experiencing some anxiety.

Mental stim. does not need to be rocket-science, but it does require some knowledge of what dogs really are as a spe-cies—creative and commonsensical. We will take advantage of our dog's five senses in order to provide them with this important benefit to a good quality of life. Most of the training and ideas for mental stimulation in this guide stem from the facts that dogs are:

- ▶ Predators, scavengers & opportunistic feeders.
- ▶ They investigate and enjoy the world mostly through their noses.
- ▶ Highly social animals.

▶ Bond with their social group (if they can trust it).

▶ Enjoy engagement with their environment and solving puzzles.

▶ Safety is their #1 concern.

▶ They do not *fake* pain or discomfort to manipulate us. They are pretty transparent in how they are feeling.

Training & Feeding Routines For Mental Stimulation

I want to remind you that the goals of this guide are to provide you with recommendations and ideas so that you can give your dog something to occupy its mind and pass the time while recuperating. Not only will it make things so much easier for your dog, but it will make the constant management so much easier for you too!

While it is great to take opportunities like this to end with a very well trained dog as a result of weeks of confinement, the most important takeaway is to keep your dog safe. You can do this by following your veterinarian's recommendations, and providing much needed enrichment for your dog so that he does not fall into

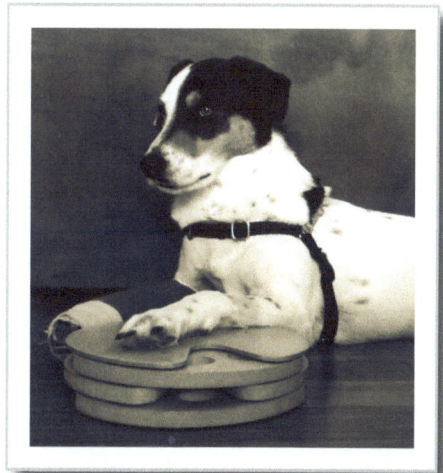

Food dispensing toys are a great way to provide mental stimulation. They come in a variety of shapes and skill levels.

a depressive state (yes, dogs can suffer from depression too!) Your dog can become out of control or anxious as a result of not having any or only a few appropriate outlets for physical as well as mental engagement.

The fact that our dogs cannot understand that this "new" life for them is not permanent can most definitively add to their distress. We understand the reasons behind the needed surgery, but your dog does not understand why suddenly his life is so different. Lack of control over ones' circumstances is one of the most detrimental aspects of well-being. This is, in part, what makes this sort of recuperation so taxing for the dog as they do not understand why they cannot do what they used to do before the surgery, and frankly it is also one of the hardest things for folks too. Unfortunately, this is not something our dogs can understand.

What To Train Before The Surgery

If your dog has learned the following skills before the surgery, it will make management of your dog much easier to accomplish.

1   Comfortably being in the crate.
2   Loose leash walking.
3   *Wait*! Defined as your dog not crossing a threshold such as running past a door, jumping out of the car or even the door of his X-pen or crate.

4 Acceptance — or better yet enjoying wearing the Elizabethan collar (the plastic cone dogs are required to wear when they should not disturb the site of surgery).

5 Eating effectively out of food-dispensing toys such as Kongs®.

6 Lying down on verbal cue.

7 Walking up and down a ramp so that your dog can get in and out of the car safely if you cannot lift your dog because he is too heavy for you to lift.

8 *"Leave it"* — meaning your dog will stop interacting with anything we do not want the dog to interact with. This could be another dog on leash, trash on the ground or for our purposes here, the site of surgery.

What To Train While Recuperating

Most of the training plans here are meant to provide enrichment. It really does not matter if you reach the goal of the training plan per se. If you do, awesome, it means both of you had lots of practice and your dog's recuperation was less boring. Of course, if you were not able to teach the behaviors as suggested above prior to surgery, you can still tackle them. The only two that I would suggest clearing with your veterinarian is the walking up or down the ramp and "settle". Please do not attempt this if your Vet has not cleared you to do so, your dog may fall or you can just make things worse.

Also, keep in mind, that the whole point of working on the training plans before the surgery is for you and your dog to practice while he is lying low. The dog will reach higher levels of performance and again things will be much smoother for you and your dog during the recuperation process. The behaviors listed below will help in giving your dog some mental stimulation as well as helping you in the management of your dog.

▶ Settle (a shaping exercise: the dog lies on his side with his head on the floor).
▶ Puzzle games (most dogs will need some direction on how to work the puzzle toy).
▶ Sit & stay or down & stay.

The training sessions are meant to be short. Between 3-5 minutes in length. Of course, you can do as many sessions as you and your dog can muster. For most of the behaviors you will need more than one session to teach it effectively to your dog. And that is okay!

BEFORE each session please do the following:

1   Be ready with what you need: clicker, treats, bed, leash handy.
2   Review the Push, Drop, Stick system so that your dog is getting feedback and being successful. See Chapter 1 of this guide.
3   Read the training plan so you know the order of steps.

4   Remember your goals for the session: Mental stim. for your dog & having fun.

Training Plans

NOTE:

You can watch videos of most of the training plans on the **Get Well Soon!** YouTube channel.

Crate Training

The process of teaching dogs to love their crates can be easy or an arduous one depending on how it is done and the dog's previous experience or association with the crate. Your goal then is to create only positive associations between the crate and your dog. Remember that the crate should be ample enough for the dog to be able to stand on all four feet comfortably, to lie down and turn around so that he truly has freedom of movement. Let's begin the crate training.

1   Begin by placing the crate in a high-traffic area so that your dog feels comfortable investigating it.

2   Feed your dog either next to the crate or just inside the crate- if she has not had a previous bad association with the crate. Make sure the door is left open and your dog can go in and out.

3   Place some high value treats inside the crate; leave the door open for your dog to find them. Do this several times for a few days. Continue to feed the meal next to the crate or inside by moving the food bowl a little more towards the back of the crate. Take it slow! If you rush your dog might regress.

4   Once your dog is eating happily inside the crate with the food bowl all the way inside with the door open, then...

5   Close the door while your dog is eating inside the crate all the way in. Remain nearby.

6   After your dog has finished his meal, let your dog out without too much fanfare. Repeat as many times/days as needed for your dog to be eating without minding the door being closed.

7   Slowly you will add time to your dog remaining inside the crate with the door closed and you nearby.

8   Present a really good bone or chewy inside the crate.

9   Ask your dog to go in, give him the bone and close the crate.

10 Remain in the room and praise your dog if you think this will help your dog relax.

If your dog is not able to remain quiet, relaxed even lying down and without barking, whining or pawing the door in an attempt to be let out means that either:

▶ You went too fast on the previous steps. So, you need to go back to easy steps until your pup is successful.

▶ Also, it could be that your dog is not interested in what you are presenting at that time. Try again with something different and see if your dog appears more interested and willing to get inside the crate on her own.

Slowly increase the time your dog remains inside the crate with a safe chewy or a stuffed Kong. Remember, that when we skip steps or we push too hard the dog regresses.

If your pup is now happy, relaxed (most likely lying down) and enjoying the Kong inside the crate:

1   Begin to exit the room or the home for a few minutes. Make sure to come back before your dog is done extracting the food from the toy.

2   Slowly continue to add 1 minute at a time. I know it sounds daunting but the minutes will add up fast and your dog will be properly and humanely crate trained. Alternatively, you can place the crate next to you when watching a movie, reading or having dinner, and treating your dog one morsel at a time. Instead of food, you can give him a chew toy. This is a very reliable way to add duration with your dog inside the crate because he has your company while enjoying something he likes.

3   As your dog continues to enjoy being in the crate-- because only good stuff happens while in the crate--you can begin to leave your dog in the crate. Before putting him in the crate make sure he has an opportunity to empty the

bladder and had some mental stimulation. This way your dog is ready to go into his crate and relax.

Loose Leash Walking

Below are a few measures to teach your dog not to pull on the leash. You might find that one of them works best, or you can use more than one of the techniques below as well. Please keep in mind that everyone who walks the dog should focus on having your dog not pulling on the leash, otherwise it will be much more difficult to teach them to walk nicely on leash.

If your dog pulls and the leash is taut, you will:

1 STOP walking!
2 Take a couple of steps behind your dog and to either side. Most likely your dog will see your movement with its periphery vision and turn back towards you.
3 Call your dog to you (ideally your dog will come to you by your side—as in a heel position). Once she does...
4 WAIT for a few seconds (literally count three seconds in your head) and then deliver a...
5 treat or allow your dog to continue walking on a loose leash, or to go sniff an interesting spot.

The procedure above should be practiced first inside the home or in a non-distracting environment before practicing with distractions. Distractions are anything that interest your dog while on a walk and that encourage pulling. Once you are both successful in a low distraction environment, practice with distractions you might find on your walk.

NOTE:

- ▶ It is okay to call your his name to get the dog's attention and then proceed with the steps.
- ▶ It's also okay to re-direct your pup by asking him/her to walk with you in a new direction by using a verbal cue such as "this way."
- ▶ Initially when walking with your dog you can go back and forth between clipping your dog on a FRONT clip harness when you are not focusing on the loose leash walking techniques above, and clipping to the collar when practicing the techniques above. In time, the amount of time you are practicing with your dog, your dog's ability to respond should improve so that the entirety of the walk is done with your dog walking on a loose leash on either the flat collar or a front clip harness.

Teaching Wait!

Door dashing is a favorite sport of most dogs. It's just so exciting to get to the other side. But in addition to irritating us, it can also be dangerous. Sometimes, what is on the other side is a busy street. The *wait* cue teaches your dog to pause or stop at the doorway, or any other threshold, until you give the "all clear." Besides keeping your dog safe, "waiting" teaches dogs self-control.

In my definition "wait" is different from "stay." "Wait" means that the dog should not cross a threshold such as dashing past a door, jumping off of the car, or moving forward on a trail. However, in my definition of "wait" the dog can return back to me—if we are hiking, for example, but not move ahead.

1   At the door, tell your dog, *"wait"* in a cheerful tone of voice.
2   Begin to open the door SLIGHTLY. If your dog starts to move to go out, close the door. It is also very clear to the dog and thus useful to block the exit with your body.
3   Say *"wait"* to your dog again and open the door slightly.
4   If your dog starts to move to go out, close the door again.
5   When your dog hesitates, and stands/sits in place, click (if using a clicker) and release your dog to go outside.
6   At first, remember to only open the door a few inches so your dog can't rush out. As your dog gets better, you can then open the door a little more.
7   However, as you open the door wider and wider you will ask your dog to remain in place without moving forward for LESS amount of time.
8   Begin by requesting your dog to stay put for 1-2 sec (count in your head).
9   Ask your dog to wait at every door, every time. Remember that practice makes permanent!

Practice using the cue "wait" in all these circumstances:

- ▶ All doors (even ones that lead into safe places like your backyard).
- ▶ Sidewalk curb.
- ▶ Getting in and out of cars.
- ▶ During off–leash hikes. Dog waits before you release her to go play or does not move forward until you give your release cue.

Comfort With The *Elizabethan* Collar Or A Muzzle

If you teach your dog prior to the surgery to be comfortable with the Elizabethan collar or a muzzle, you will really be helping your dog out. I have never met a dog that is comfortable wearing an Elizabethan collar, but unfortunately there is nothing else that can prevent your dog from disturbing the site of surgery. If you think a muzzle will be less aversive to your dog, or your dog is already comfortable with one, please make sure it is only a BASKET muzzle. If you prefer your dog uses a basket muzzle instead of an Elizabethan collar, check with your Vet first.

A basket muzzle has several openings and your dog can open its mouth to breath and pant. CAUTION: A "groomer's" muzzle does *not* provide the dog the opportunity to pant and should only be used for a very short time and while the dog is stationary such at a groomer's or a visit to the vet. Keep it safe and only use a basket muzzle that is fitted correctly on your dog. The muzzle should sit on your dog's nose but not so high up that it's too close to his eyes. It should be tight in the back so that the dog cannot pull it down.

The nose should fit comfortably inside. If the nose appears to shorten or bunch up inside, then the muzzle is too small for your dog.

Introducing The Elizabethan Collar Or Muzzle.

Basket Muzzle

To make your dog associate the Elizabethan collar or muzzle with good things, get out the yummiest treats you can think of, and follow the steps below. The steps can be done in one session or over several, depending on your dog's comfort level.

Reach through and treat

1 Hold the collar/muzzle up with one hand so your dog notices it.
2 Feed your dog while he is looking at the muzzle in your hand.
3 Repeat 3-6 times.
4 From now on, every time your dog sees the collar/muzzle, treat him. When the collar or muzzle is out of sight from your dog, **stop** treating.

Nose in the muzzle for treat

1   Cup the muzzle or hold the collar with one hand. Hold the treat so your dog has to put his nose *into* or through the muzzle/collar to get the treat.
2   As soon as the treat is gone, remove the muzzle or collar.
3   Repeat until your dog voluntarily sticks his nose into the muzzle or through the collar to get the treat.
4   Now treat several times really quickly so your dog keeps his face in the muzzle/collar for 2-3 seconds.
5   Repeat until the dog can keep the muzzle/collar on for 10 seconds with you delivering a treat every few seconds.

Nose in the muzzle and buckle for treat

1   Load the muzzle up with treats or have lots of treats in your hand (or throw them on the floor) once you have the collar on your dog. While your dog eats, hold the neck straps behind his neck and apply light pressure. As soon as he finishes the treats, take off the muzzle or collar.
2   Next, have your dog put his nose in the muzzle before you deliver treats.
3   Hold the neck straps, then start feeding the treats through the muzzle or the collar.

Adding Duration

1 Repeat this exercise until your dog keeps his head in the muzzle for 3-5 seconds *before* you start treating.
2 Have your dog put his nose in the muzzle, but now close the buckle or cord for the collar and unleash a bunch of preferably extra delicious treats. When the treats are gone, take off the muzzle/collar.

Wearing the muzzle or collar on a walk

1 Put the muzzle or the collar on and immediately take your dog for a fun walk. Take some treats with you and dish them out along the way.
2 If your dog tries to remove the muzzle by pawing at it or lowering to the ground, *gently* and with a happy voice, encourage your dog to come along as you raise the leash a bit to prevent him from removing the muzzle. If the dog persists, you might have to go back to the at home exercise until you can tell that the dog expects to get a treat after seeing the collar or muzzle, and that your dog is really relaxed when wearing it at home. Be patient and consistent as this might take some time.

FOOD DISPENSING TOYS — KONGS

Dogs are genetically programmed to hunt for their food. By feeding your dog out of a food dispensing toy, such as a KONG®, you will be providing your dog with excellent mental stimulation! Kong is the brand name for many really great toys that serve this purpose. However, their original toy the KONG, a spiral-like cone made of hard rubber that is hollow, can be filled with your dog's full

The original Kong toy

meal. This is my go-to toy. You can, of course, mix and match toys to feed your dog. Another brand of toys that can be used in this same manner is the *Squirrel Dude* by Premier.

There are other types of toys appropriate to use with dry kibble. It is also worth mentioning the Manners *Minder* is a gadget that dispenses kibble or treats shaped like most kibble, and per your programming you can literally serve your dog's meal while you are gone. Plus, your dog has something fun to do. The sky is truly the limit when it comes to food dispensing toys.

Stuffing Suggestions for KONG Toy or Squirrel Dude

Keep in mind that your dog is learning a new skill so it might take a few tries for your pup to get excited and able to extract the food out of the toy. Do not give up! Instead, continue to encourage the use of it if you notice that your dog is not interested or struggling. Make it easier for the dog to be successful by using the tips below. As your dog becomes more adept in extracting the food, you can make it more challenging and fun. Below are some ideas as to how to make the extracting of the food more challenging once your dog has mastered the previous step.

Teaching Level

1 Fill a size-appropriate KONG® for your dog with kibble or your dog's food.
2 Give the toy to your dog for her to experiment getting the food out of it by rotating it, pawing it,
3 At this level, it's okay to encourage your dog or even help her a bit by rotating the KONG® yourself so food comes out.

Beginner's Level

Make the extracting of the food a bit harder by stuffing the KONG and then placing a harder item, such as a piece of jerky, dry liver or a banana chip to block the kibble from falling out freely.

Advanced Level 1

1 Increase the level of difficult by wetting the kibble ahead of time so that it swells and becomes "mushy." You can wet with water or something special such as chicken broth.
2 Feed your dog the whole meal out of KONGS once your dog is adept at getting all the food out and appears to enjoy the activity. Yes, you need to buy several KONGS to accommodate the whole meal.

Advanced Level 2 /Summer Days

1. Prepare KONG® as you did for previous levels, and then freeze overnight or for a few hours.
2. Allow KONG® to thaw for about 1 hour before serving.
3. Best to serve in a crate or outside to avoid a possible mess.

Recipe Examples Courtesy Of Jean Donaldson, From *The Academy For Dog Trainers*

Tight Version (more advanced) Stuffing

1. Layer 1 (deepest): mild cheese chunks, freeze dried liver bits.
2. Layer 2: dog kibble, cookies or Liver Biscotti, Cheerios, sugar-free/salt-free peanut butter, dried banana chips.
3. Layer 3: baby carrot stick(s), turkey and/or leftover ravioli or tortellini, dried apples, dried apricots.
4. Pack as tightly as possible into the Kong. The last item in should be a dried apricot or piece of ravioli, presenting a smooth "finish" under the main hole.

"Lite" Version:

- Substitute crumbled rice cake; for freeze-dried liver, substitute Caesar croutons; for peanut butter substitute fat-free cream cheese.
- The goal is to feed your dog at least one of his daily meals via a food dispensing toy or several different toys.

Walking Up & Down A Ramp to Get Inside The Car Or Use The Stairs

Some dogs will find this exercise really easy and nothing to be concerned about. For others, it could represent a real challenge. Dogs, just like people, might not feel comfortable when they think they might lose their balance or when there is elevation involved.

- ▶ If your dog appears comfortable approaching your car when the ramp is fully extended, you may place some treats on the ramp (do not feed by mouth as this might make your dog lose its balance) making a trail of treats up the ramp.
- ▶ Use lots of praise and happy talk.
- ▶ Repeat once again with your dog coming down the ramp.
- ▶ Use "*wait*" as a verbal cue if your dog has already learned what this means to ensure your dog will walk calmly down the ramp.

For dogs hesitant about walking up or down the ramp, follow the steps below:

1 Let your dog investigate the ramp when the ramp is just lying on the ground and away from the car.
2 Click and treat your dog for **any** investigation of the ramp such as: looking in the direction of the ramp, sniffing, licking or walking towards it.

3   Then set up the ramp as if it's going to be used by your dog. Make sure it is secure!!

4   Begin walking your pup towards the ramp.

5   Encourage again *any* movement towards the ramp using the click and treats; encourage your dog by talking to him happily.

6   Continue as long as your dog wants to move forward. Always paying on the ramp, instead of feeding your dog in the mouth. If for any reason your dog hesitates or stops wanting to go up the ramp, do **not force** your dog. Instead, end the session and begin again another time. If we respect our dog's learning process, we will keep his trust in us intact and with a few more repetitions his confidence will soar. Please know that your dog is not being dominant, stubborn or stupid. Dogs can struggle with new learning just as we do.

NOTE:

Make sure you first clear with your Vet before teaching your dog this exercise if he has already had the surgery.

What To Train When Your Dog Is Recuperating

The behaviors in this section could also be trained prior to your dog's surgery. It all depends how much time you have to do so. However, the suggested behaviors to train *prior* to the surgery are behaviors that your dog will *not* be able to execute with ease and safety after surgery or that will really make a difference in your ability to keep your dog content and not bored while recuperating. The training plans that follow will provide your dog with mental stimulation in a safe manner while recuperating.

Lie Down

1 Lure your dog into a down (from a sit).
2 Place a treat in front of your dog's front paws.
3 Click and deliver a treat for lowering the head/neck.
4 Click and deliver a treat for bending the elbows.
5 Click and treat for bending of the knees.
6 Treat for going all the way down and resting the belly on the ground.

Use Of An Empty Hand Signal

After your dog has been successful with a food lure, you need to move on to an **empty** *hand cue so that your dog learns to work first and then get paid. Some dogs will hesitate at this juncture.* If this is the case with your dog, ask your dog for a behavior that she has already learned and pay her for that in order to keep her interested in working with you, then go back and ask for the lying down with an empty hand signal. This is one of the main problems with people using food while training; they fail to remove the food promptly after the dog has been successful for a few trials with the food. Your dog needs to trust that you will pay after the behavior and not become dependent on seeing the treat first in order to perform.

1 Remove the treat from your hand and with an EMPTY hand...

2 Give your dog the EXACT same hand signal you did while holding food in your hand. Your dog might hesitate at this point. Be patient and persevere!

3 Click and reward your dog for lowering the elbows, knees or even the neck at this point.

4 Pay your dog for approximations of the behavior such as lowering to the ground certain body parts.

5 Once your dog is lowering his belly all the way to the ground and has done this consistently for 5 trials you can move to on to the next step.

INTRODUCING THE VERBAL CUE

▶ When using a verbal cue AND a hand signal, it is CRUCIAL that you first give the dog the hand signal.

▶ Followed by the verbal cue and not both at the same time. Dogs will default to minding our body language over verbal cues so if you give both of them at the same time (hand signal and verbal cue) your dog will not learn the verbal cue.

▶ Once your dog is fluent in lying down when you ask him to do so, you can ask with abandonment.

▶ Occasionally treat your dog for lying down, otherwise the behavior will go into extinction.

Sit & Stay Or Lie Down & Stay

This training plan can be used also for a sit/stay. You can, of course, practice both body positions. "Stay" means that your dog is able to maintain a given position for a certain amount of time. If your dog is constantly breaking the position it means that you are asking for too much too soon. Go back to making things easy (less time on the position) and build the time slowly. Duration is much harder for dogs to execute well so be patient.

1. Have your dog sitting or in a down position in front of you.
2. Say your dog's name followed by a "stay" cue. You can use a hand signal, but remember that the hand signal comes before the verbal and not at the same time.
3. Begin by taking one mini-step to the right as you are facing your dog and are standing close to him.
4. Return to your dog if its butt (or belly for a "down") remains on the ground; click and treat.
5. Continue adding steps—up to three steps on this same side, repeat for five trials and follow the PDS system to move forward or not.
6. Step now at a 45-degree angle from your dog as you are facing the dog and repeat for five trials and follow the PDS system to move forward or not.
7. If your dog remains in place with you moving two to three steps to the side and at the 45-degree angle go to the second side (do NOT go around your dog just yet).

8   Repeat the sequence by moving to the side as you are facing your dog; up to three steps once your dog can stay put when you move up to three steps to the side.

9   Step to a 45-degree angle as you are facing your dog.

10 Return to face your dog.

11 Click and treat while facing the dog repeat for five trials.

Going Behind

1   Begin to go behind/around your pup on your first side.

2   Once your dog can stay with its butt or belly on the ground as you go around.

3   Come back to face your dog and click and treat.

4   Practice now going around your dog on the second side.

If your dog breaks the sit/stay or down/stay, reposition your dog on the down or the sit and go back to the step you were working on. Remember, if your dog fails two times in a row, go back drop the criteria to make things easier. We want your pup to get it right so that we can pay him!

Moving Forward

You can continue to add levels of difficulty by moving away from your dog by starting with 1 to 2 steps away. Repeat the sequence above but a bit farther from your dog. So, that you know, adding distance between you and your dog will indeed present a more difficult scenario for your dog. Plan accordingly by going back to working next to your dog should he fail two times in a row.

Occasionally treat your dog for staying in place, otherwise the behavior will go into extinction.

Leave It

Teaching a dog to stop interacting with a myriad of things is a very useful behavior for your dog to learn. It will come in handy when your dog is not supposed to run after a squirrel or even say hello to a dog friend while your dog is taking some down time. I used the "leave it" cue when I needed Rio to stop licking her cast whenever she was taking a break from the Elizabethan collar.

1 Begin to teach "leave it" by presenting a closed fist with treat inside approximately 3-4" away from dog's nose/mouth.
2 The second your dog stops interacting with your closed fist, click and pay the dog from your hand.
3 Repeat for five trials.
4 Once your dog is successful, push the criteria- (per our Push, Drop, Stick system).

Presenting a *partially* open fist.

1 Present the partially open fist a bit farther from your dog's nose.
2 The nano-second your dog stops interacting with your fist, click and deliver the food.
3 Practice for FIVE trials using Push, Drop, Stick again.

Adding Duration

▶ When your dog has gotten 5 out of 5 correct responses, make things a bit harder for your dog by:

Adding more time; one SECOND at a time to the presentation of a partially open fist so that your dog has to exercise self-control and wait longer before taking the treat that's partially visible.

You want to go up to at least FIVE seconds of duration of presenting a treat before you introduce the verbal cue...

Introducing the Verbal Cue "Leave it"

At this point, we will introduce the verbal cue. It is really important that you first say the verbal cue and after a couple of seconds (count in your head for 2 seconds) present the closed fist as you did above. Once you have done this for five trials, you can "push" to an open hand AFTER having given your dog the verbal cue.

NOTE:

It is crucial that you do not reach for the treat prior to giving the verbal cue; this will only distract your dog. Remain as neutral as possible in your body language. Say your verbal cue and after a couple of seconds present your fist with the food.

Moving Forward

You can then try the same routine by presenting your dog a favorite toy, ball, chew bone. Dogs do not generalize well which means they do not understand that "leave it," in our example above, applies to different items or circumstances such as when your dog is licking its cast. On occasion treat your dog for *"leaving" things* you don't want her to have, otherwise the behavior will go into extinction.

Settle

Please **check with your DVM before attempting to teach "settle" with your dog.** Depending on the condition of your dog if this is a good thing to teach your pup at this time. Please use common sense when asking your dog to rotate any part of his body as described in the plan below. It should be a comfortable and not force rotation of the hips.

This particular training plan is a great way of not only having some fun with your dog while she learns this, but it will also teach your dog to relax. It might be very difficult for your dog to be able to really relax when it is already spending so much time in a crate or X-pen. Teaching the body to be relaxed will help in keeping your dog's mental state also relaxed.

We will train the "settle" behavior in small steps by using approximations of behavior. Depending on where you are training, you will not be able to train with your dog while he is inside his crate. You might need to attach a leash to your dog and to your waist so that your dog does not have an opportunity to bolt.

1 With your dog lying down, next to you and you sitting to your dog's side ...

2 With a treat in your hand, lure your dog by putting the treat to his nose.

3 Move the treat slowly from your dog's nose to the back of his spine as if you were tracing an arc from nose to back.

4 Click and treat when your dog is turning the head/neck. With each repetition, you want to see your dog safely turning his neck more and more.

5 If you are not sure this side is easiest for your dog to drop its hips to the ground, lure your dog on the other side. Once you know which side is easier for your dog:

6 Click and treat for a *slight* lift of the front leg on the same side the neck is turning as the hips are dropping to the opposite side.

7 Repeat until your dog is lying on its side.

8 Click and treat your dog for placing the side of its head on the ground.

9 Click and treat your dog while he is lying on the ground.

10 Introduce the verbal cue. Remember to first say the cue "*settle*" and "wait" for a minimum of two seconds before you lure your dog.

11 Repeat until your dog is lying down on its side on hearing your **verbal** cue alone.

12 Now you can use it when you need your dog to relax further.

13 Occasionally treat your dog for s*ettling*; otherwise the behavior will go into extinction.

CHAPTER 5

Additional Recommendations For Mental Stimulation

O NE OF MY favorite things to do is coming up with viable and efficient ways to mentally stimulate dogs. It is, of course, more of a challenge when our dog is limited by what he should be doing. The good news is that even small things can make a real big difference in the quality of your dog's life while she is lying low after surgery. I like to think of mental stimulation as a multipronged approach by introducing different strategies such as training and management tools that welcomes flexibility in the activities presented to our dog.

Chewing

Chewing is one of the most favorite natural behaviors for dogs. For this reason, we must give our dog ample opportunities for this activity. What to chew is also a matter of preference for the dog. Just like some people enjoy reading poetry and others spy novels. You might have to experiment a bit and give your dog some time to try different options. Whatever you provide your dog to chew, it must be something that you do not mind your dog chewing on. If you offer him what you think is an "old" shoe, he might not necessarily differentiate which shoes are okay to chew on and which are not.

In addition, you must observe your dog's chewing habits. Some dogs will want to swallow big chunks of whatever they are chewing, while others are more careful and almost dainty in how they approach this activity.

Please check with your veterinarian as to what the best choice is for your dog. I have never had an incident with any of my dogs chewing what I regularly provide to them, but indeed dogs are all individual, so common sense and some prior observation is a good rule of thumb. When left alone, my approach entails giving my dogs to what I consider to be very safe items, such as a Kong toy. Only when I am around to supervise do I provide potentially risky items.

Items Most Dogs Enjoy Chewing

1 **Edibles**: Chew bones, pigs' ears, bully sticks, greenies, raw hides
2 **Non-Edibles**: Tennis balls, Nyla bones, Kongs (without food)
3 **Dissectible Things**: Plush toys, rope toys, Hide-A-Bee (Squirrel, Bird)
4 **Puzzle Toys**: Stuffed Kong, stuffed marrowbone, tricky treat balls

My Personal Favorite Items

- ▶ Flat rawhides (I DO NOT recommend rawhide bones, but you might want to talk to your vet about this). Rawhides are not as digestible as other chew items are, and there is also the potential for your dog to consume a big enough piece and choke. I think the *flat* rawhide chips are a good alternative.
- ▶ Bully sticks: Dogs love them! More digestible than the rawhide. I think of these as dessert and give them to my dogs every night. You can buy locally or online (see resources) as prices can vary considerably.
- ▶ Marrow bones: This is the bone with a center hole that contains meat inside. Once emptied by your dog, you can refill it with some high value stuff such as sardines (really!—they are great for dogs), baby food. Remember that freezing marrow bones can give your dog top mental

stimulation. Make sure you buy the right size bone for your dog. You do not want your dog putting the whole bone in his mouth at once and that you throw out any bone that appears to have splintered.

▶ Last but not least, any hard-rubber toy that I can stuff with sardines, boiled egg, or similar goodies. My dogs really think I'm a great cook!

Visual Ways to Stimulate

"Hands down," car rides are a fantastic activity option for dogs that can't move, but can still ride and enjoy riding in a car. If your dog likes this activity before you both go driving be absolutely sure the temperatures are not too hot — by hot I mean temperatures higher than 70° F. In the car, the temperature is always higher than the outside air, so use 70 as a benchmark. Contrary to popular belief, having the windows open is not enough to cool a dog in a car. WARNING! DOGS DIE OF HEAT EXPOSURE EVERY YEAR. It is your responsibility to keep your dog safe. One really good option is to find covered parking so that your pup can be cool and safe, or skip the ride IF you plan to get out of the car and intend to leave your dog in it.

If the temperature drops to 50° F and below, I will consider taking my dog in the car but I will put a coat on my dog. It's not the same to be active and warm when it is cold as it is to lie inside a cold car for long stretches.

NOTE:

If the temperatures are so cold that it's dangerous for a person to be outside, then I suggest you keep your dog inside. Or go for a car ride, but remain in the car with your dog and the heater on.

I'm aware that dogs love to stick their heads out the window to take in smells and sights, but do not allow this. Your dog does not know better. Your dog can have a strange object get into its eye or nose cavity, or he can fall out of the window. Sometimes in life we need to choose safety and common sense over fun; in my view this is one of those times. Of course, you can lower the window some so that your dog gets to sniff the air as long as the dog's head remains in the car.

Visits From Friends

If your dog is a social butterfly towards people, having someone drop by to say hello can be a really cool thing for both of you. You still need to plan ahead if your dog is one of those that *loooooveees* to jump up to greet visitors. I suggest thinking ahead about your friend's arrival, and where your dog should be to avoid too much excitement.

Passive Visual Stimulation

By passive stimulation I mean that the environment is providing some enrichment for your dog.

Place one of your dog's many crates or X-pens next to a window where there is **some activity** outside. For some dogs, looking out the window it's like going to the outside cinema. Not all dogs can tolerate this. You'll need to try this activity out when you're around so that you can make sure your pup is not getting too wound up by constant foot traffic, or too much noise, if your dog cannot handle this, try putting your dog near another window location where perhaps you can hang a bird feeder or put him in a room with a mobile on the ceiling.

Dissecting "Stuff"

Because dogs are predators, they dissect their food as part of the chain of behaviors in the predatory sequence. True, our pet dogs are not hunting nowadays to eat, but they are still wired with this particular trait. When we use natural behaviors to stimulate our dog's brain everyone wins. Dissecting requires shredding to pieces pretty much anything that you don't mind your dog destroying and that your dog will not get injured in during the process. Some dogs (think Labs) love to put all sorts of items in their mouths; and many will swallow almost any item presented to them. If your dog has a history of consuming anything in sight, you need to watch the dog carefully as it engages in dissecting.

Favorite items to dissect:

- ▶ Newspapers, magazines, cardboard boxes (makes sure there are no staples and that the cardboard is not too hard for your dog).
- ▶ Fabrics, old towels, pillowcases.
- ▶ Toys, of course, many dogs dissect their own toys. You can, however, provide other items that are acceptable from the list above so that when you give your dog an expensive toy, you can re-direct your pup if he begins to destroy it.

To make the dissecting activity more interesting for your dog, you can hide some tasty treats in the box or pillowcase and witness your dog going wild! This activity can be done inside the X-pen and potentially even in the crate, depending on your dog's interest and the item you are giving your dog. Experiment a little here.

Licking Bowls

Rio enjoys licking a plate from our dinner.

Yep. Even licking a plate used for oatmeal, eggs or any other food item that is appropriate for your dog to consume is fair game. Keep in mind once again, that what we are after is variety since dogs thrive in consistency sprinkled with novelty, and not necessarily how long the activity last as in the case of licking a bowl for a few seconds. At the end of the day, small things like this do add up.

Popcorn Or Bubble "Party"

I don't know about your household, but in mine, we are all popcorn lovers—almost to the point of obsession.

My dogs and I regularly share some popcorn. If your dog can control itself and refrain from too much movement you could throw a popcorn or bubble *party*. In essence, your dog gets to go after the popcorn that you are freely throwing into his containment area. Keep the throwing of popcorn or bubbles somewhat subdued if you suspect your dog might get too excited. But if this is not the case, then encourage your dog by using a happy-tone of voice as he shows you the skills of going after the popcorn or bubbles.

Simple Soothing Ideas

As we experience the world visually, dogs experience their surroundings through their noses and their very powerful sense of smell. Arm yourself with some cotton balls and wet them with some different and interesting smells for your dog or just present the item itself for sniffing.

Some things to try could be lavender, coconut oil, chicken or beef stock, banana, apples, a bird's feather, leather glove, or wool. The goal is just to give your dog a moment of smelling something specific. Perhaps something your dog already likes or it could be a new smell. Be mindful not to present items that by default are too strong for your dog, such as pepper and any spicy stuff. You can just gather your items and present one at a time. If you notice your dog is curious about a particular one, give it another pass. You can continue to add items as you think of them.

Gentle Bodywork

Dogs, just like us, can get into patterns of movement or even rest that produces aches and stiffness. Touching your dog in general and in particular, when given canine bodywork is really a fantastic complement to aid your dog in recovering and feeling better overall. Of course, some dogs do not enjoy being touched; if this is the case for your dog, clearly this is not a good idea.

If you can afford having a professional come work with your dog perhaps once a week that would be very beneficial. Alternatively, you can learn some simple techniques to give your dog some release from too much lying around. Do keep in mind that petting, while being a form of touch and has proven to have benefits for both parties, does not produce the same benefits as massage, or TTouch® or even what is often referred as "energy" work.

Tellington TTouch®

As a Tellington TTouch practitioner, I often incorporate this method in my dog training practice. While your dog will not be able to do the groundwork, which is a variety of exercises with simple equipment, you can still provide him with the benefits of TTouch.

In essence, TTouch is a method of working with animals that has proven effective in reducing stress, fear, aggression and anxiety; as well as modifying behavior, and when combined with veterinary care, can aid in recovery from surgery. The approach is gentle, yet systematic and can help animals to better cope with different and novel situations.

TTouch employs the use of gentle touches, body wraps and groundwork. These modalities engage and support the dog's nervous system. When we work with the nervous system in this manner, we can teach the dog to move in non-habitual ways.

Another wonderful benefit of T Touch is that anyone can learn the touches. You can watch some resourceful videos on how to perform the T Touches through their website: www.ttouch.com. Their books are also full of excellent illustrations and guidance.

CHAPTER 6

More Than One Dog At Home

HOUSEHOLDS WITH MORE than one dog can prove to be more challenging for the dog who is recuperating from surgery. Or his life can be more fun and easy if he and the other dog are good friends. Regardless, every household is unique when it comes to how dogs interact with each other. Their life stages, their likes and dislikes, and their day-to-day activities. All these characteristics need to be considered in order to make good choices for the dogs, but perhaps more importantly for the dog who's in recovery.

Planning Ahead

If you plan your day ahead, life with your convalescent dog will be less stressful for both of you. Having more than one person in the household can help with dog care and will take some of the burden off the individual managing the dog's routine. It's important, however; to determine who will be responsible for the specific chores surroundings the dogs. Who will be doing the feedings? For exercising the non–convalescent dog(s) and mentally stimulating them all. For this reason, I suggest:

> ▶ Having a calendar and clear communication as to who is doing *what* and *when*-- will keep things running smoothly.
> ▶ I cannot stress enough the importance of getting competent help or even a reliable friend who can exercise your other dog, or drop him off at daycare.

Whether you have help or will do all the caregiving on your own, I recommend the following:

Routine

> ▶ Keep your dog's daily routine as intact as possible.

Dog Play

> ▶ Do realize that if your dogs are playmates, now you have one that cannot play and another one that is wanting to

do so. Can you think of an activity that can take the place of dog play? Are there other dogs in the neighborhood your other dogs are 'friends' with? Is your healthy dog comfortable enough to go to a reputable daycare perhaps once or twice a week?

Play Fair

▶ All dogs need your attention and time, not only the one that is convalescing. Depending on your dog's specific situation, there might be activities that all your dogs enjoy doing together and which they might still be able to do as a group. This includes car rides, lying on the sofa with you — if your dogs are allowed on the sofa —, puzzle toys in separate areas of the home, or a chewing bone.

Take Advantage of Feeding Times

One of the strategies that has worked for me over the years is to think of feeding times as perfect opportunities to train the dogs; be it a client's dog that is staying with us for board and training, or in the most recent case with my dog Rio. Rio would get her breakfast in a Kong while I took Deuce out to play with the ball. Rio stayed busy with the Kong as Deuce and I made our way out the door.

NOTE:

I have known of dogs that will pick a fight with their other household companion who returns from a prolonged vet visit or surgery. Clearly, this is a situation that you want to avoid. It's possible that the healthy dog finds the smell on the other dog unsettling. Perhaps the dog in recovery appears "weak" or just different; especially if wearing a cast, or Elizabethan collar or other health aid.

In addition, your injured dog might feel very vulnerable and would much rather not have her pals come too close to her. In any event, to avoid any potential quarrels, my recommendation to avoid any potential quarrel is to keep the dogs separated by keeping your dog who's in recovery inside the X-pen or crate when she returns home from the clinic.

Ideally, you'll let your dog who's in recovery, rest before she gets to sniff her buddy through the X-pen. Monitor all your dogs and pay attention to behaviors that do not appear normal. When in doubt, play it safe, and allow everyone to adjust to the new conditions before having them interact fully.

Take Care Of Your Own Needs

> ▶ From my perspective, it's natural for us to feel sorry for our dog that is limited from fully participating in family activities. While we can't always make things exactly "right," we *can* make things a bit easier for all of our

dogs if we plan ahead so they all get something they need or want.

- ▶ Lower your expectations. The demands put on you might not allow for making sure everyone gets what they want or need at all times. Put aside your expectations for the time being and concentrate on the bigger picture to facilitate your dog's recuperation while you try and keep your sanity intact.

- ▶ Recognize that frustration and sadness are part of anyone's life- including our precious dogs. If your dog is not acting as she normally does, make sure that there is nothing seriously wrong, that she's not in pain or has an infection.

- ▶ Comfort your dog and be empathetic as you also recognize that you are doing the best you can.

I hope this guide will prove useful to you while your dog is in recovery. While it can be a daunting task to keep an otherwise healthy dog confined and with little mobility, keep in mind that there are strategies to help you through this process. If you can keep your dog safe by following your DVM's advice while at the same time engage your dog with daily mental enrichment you will find the care of your dog to be less of a burden.

And who knows, as the weeks fly by, you might even end up with a fully recovered pup who is also very well trained!

A Few Definitions

Operant Conditioning:

Animals learning about the consequences of their behavior. A type of learning controlled by consequences using reinforcement and punishment.

Stimulus:

Anything an animal can perceive with its senses.

Negative Punishment:

The REMOVAL of something the dog wants that results in a behavior decreasing.

Positive Reinforcement:

The PRESENTATION of something the dog wants/will work for that results in the behavior increasing.

Classical Conditioning:

Animals learning about patterns in the order of events around them. A learning process that occurs when two stimuli are repeatedly paired.

Motivation:

The reason(s) one has for acting or behaving in a particular way. Dogs do what's beneficial for them; we need to provide real motivation, a reason to do what we're asking.

Motivators:

Anything the dog wants at a given time. We use them to our advantage in teaching the dog to do what we want/need him to do. For example: food, play, other dogs, our attention, walks, car rides, chews etc.

Lure:

A hands-off method of guiding the dog through a behavior. For example: using a food lure to teach the dog to place its butt on the ground by raising it up over the dog's head (dog's head goes up, butt goes down).

Capturing:

Reinforcing a behavior when the dog exhibits the behavior. For example: reinforcing the dog for lying quietly on its bed.

Shaping:

Teaching by approximation. For example: teaching a dog to lie down by reinforcing when the dog lowers its head, shoulders, elbows, butt and finally the belly on the ground.

Push, Drop, Stick (PDS):

A system of counting winning/losing trials (repetitions of a behavior) in a set so that we know if we need to stay at this level of difficulty (stick) lower criteria, (drop) or raise criteria (push)

PUSH:

four or five correct responses of five trails

DROP:

one or two correct response out of five trials

STICK:

three correct responses out of five trials.

Criteria:

The exact behavior that we are reinforcing. For example: a sit-reinforce when the dog's butt hits the ground. We can observe the behavior.

Real Life Rewards (reinforcers):

Using anything that the dog wants at a given moment as a reinforcer. Food, rest, play, access to us, etc. For example: using sniffing a bush to reinforce loose leash walking.

History of Reinforcement:

How many times in the life of the dog has he been "paid" for a given <u>behavior.</u> The longer a history of reinforcement, the more <u>permanent</u> the behavior.

Clicker Training:

A technology that marks the exact discreet behavior that will be reinforced. It tells the dog reinforcement is coming his way. A clear way to communicate with our dog when used appropriately.

Management:

Changing or controlling the ENVIRONMENT (not the dog!) so that the dog does not get to practice behaviors we don't like.

Behavior Modification:

Teaching the dog an alternative behavior.

Primary Reinforcers:

Food, water, sex, social engagement and (<u>certain</u>) control over <u>environment</u>. The dog does not need to learn to want or work for these things.

Training Clean:

Good use of mechanics such as:

- ▶ Click first, then present the reinforce.
- ▶ Only say your verbal cue once. Re-set after a few seconds (10) by repeating the verbal cue.
- ▶ Present consequence **immediately** after the behavior.

Generalization:

The dog has learned and can perform a given behavior in more than one environment/setting.

Stubbornness, dominance, "knows better," feeling guilty:

Our **erroneous** reasoning as to why our dog does certain things or does not do what we want them to do.

Resources

C.H.A.C.O. Dog Training & Behavior Consulting LLC
www.chacodogtraining.com

If you are struggling with any of the advice here feel free to contact me so that I can help you.

Clicker Training
www.clickertraning.com
Great resource and ideas for future training projects.

Chewies, etc.
www.Bestbullysticks.com
www.Chewy.com
Online source for a great selection of chew items at competitive prices.

Toys

www.barkbox.com (also available at Target online)

www.cleanrun.com

Training to Become a Professional Dog Trainer

www.academyfordogtrainers.com

Online/hands on course for those wanting to become a professional dog trainer. Hands down the best program available. Also, there is a referral list of graduates.

Business Help For "Pros"

www.Dogbiz.org

Business related help for professional dog walkers & trainers. Excellent educational resource.

Products Mentioned

Treat & Train (formerly Manners Minder)

http://www.petexpertise.com/dog-training-aids/
treat-n-train-remote-dog-training.html

Training Form:

Date:

Sessions #:

Location of Session:

Steps of Training Plan Followed:

R+ (type of food used):

Next Session begin with (the next step in the training plan where you finished successfully on the prior session).

Notes:

Almudena Ortiz Cué is a graduate of the renowned San Francisco SPCA Academy for Dog Trainers (CTC), a Certified Professional Dog Trainer by the Certification Council for Professional Dog Trainers, (CPDT) a professional member of The Association of Professional Dog Trainers (APDT) and the owner of C.H.A.C.O. Dog Training & Behavior Consulting LLC, located in the Santa Fe, New Mexico area.

She is also a certified Tellington TTouch® Practitioner for Animal Companions. She was a staff trainer for two years at Tony La Russa Animal Rescue Foundation (ARF) in Walnut Creek, CA. where she worked with under-socialized dogs who had experienced lengthy shelter stays or scored poorly in the SAFER test. Her training was designed both to improve the lives of the dogs while at the shelter and to prepare them for successful adoptions. Ms. Ortiz Cué designed and implemented the shelter' first Dog Training Internship Program (Dog T.I.P.).

She is the co-author of the book: RIOJA! *The Crazy and Fun Adventures of a Smart Little Dog with Magical Powers and the Family Who Adopted Her.*